Too Much Mirch
Safia Khan

NEW**POETS**LIST

the poetry business

Published 2022 by
New Poets List
An imprint of The Poetry Business
Campo House,
54 Campo Lane,
Sheffield S1 2EG

ISBN 978-1-914914-24-9
eBook ISBN 978-1-914914-25-6
Typeset by The Poetry Business
Printed by Biddles, Sheffield

Smith|Doorstop Books are a member of Inpress:
www.inpressbooks.co.uk

Distributed by IPS UK, 1 Deltic Avenue,
Rooksley, Milton Keynes MK13 8LD

The Poetry Business gratefully acknowledges the support
of Arts Council England.

Supported using public funding by
ARTS COUNCIL
ENGLAND
LOTTERY FUNDED

Contents

For Mum and Abu

Home Invasion

Salaam, come in! Please could you take off
your shoes? Don't mind the shrapnel
studding the carpet, we keep slippers for guests.

Careful – we're always tripping over
landmines on the staircase. In fact,
we've blown ourselves to bits

so many times, we started hanging
our limbs on the washing line.
Here's the fridge, feel free to help yourself,

there's pilau rice in ice cream tubs,
and fresh hand grenades in cling film.
If you want to dry your hands,

use the caliphate flag next to the oven gloves,
we're out of kitchen towel. You probably
can't even hear me over the bloody vacuum,

someone's always trying to hoover
another war from under the carpet.
If you're cold, I can bring you a vest,

but remember, no sudden movements!
Sorry about the alarm, it's automatic –
goes off every time there's an intruder.

Debbie

Debbie follows the pampered cat when it comes to love. She pulls
the skin taut around her temples, tells me to train as a plastic surgeon
every time she sees me. The envy of Rumpelstiltskin, her scissors
spin split ends into silk. She once gave the moon a blue rinse for free.
Botox is scaffolding for her surprised eyebrows. Some pearls only
Debbie can gift: *all colours are a matter of opinion, especially caramel.*
You only get one lightning bolt love. Karma will get that nail technician,
believe you me. She is clearing her afternoon to attend a Brexit rally.
She is closing the shutters to give her hijabis some privacy. (Debbie
knows layers better than most). I think she's f*cking up my fringe, but
who am I to tell her? This is Debbie's world, we're all just living in it.

Dave

Let's discharge him today.
We're wasting a bed keeping him here,
I know a lost cause when I see one.

No need to biopsy, it's clearly end-stage.
Sadly, not much we can do at this point,
best to discharge him today.

He's asked, but don't bother with a referral
to Addiction Services – he won't engage.
Trust me, I know a lost cause when I see one.

Before you book his cab, tell him he needs
to break the cycle. Record it, otherwise
we can't discharge him today.

His notes say no fixed abode. He mentioned
a daughter. I doubt she'll take him in this state,
that's a lost cause if I've ever seen one.

Social services have called twice now.
The daughter asked why she wasn't contacted.
I said *they told me to discharge him,*
they knew a lost cause when they saw one.

On Placement

I donned mask, visor, and apron,
washed my hands the right way,

correctly identified an osteophyte
at the acromioclavicular joint,

imagined the right diagnosis,
asserted the wrong ones,

was humbled like pines after avalanche,
inspected behind the curtain,

tried not to register relief
when hers looked like mine,

translated incorrectly, blamed my parents
for speaking English in the house.

I donned mask, visor, and apron,
washed my hands the right way,

noted an antibiotic prescription
for a young wife's sudden death,

and a son's hanging decades later,
ate fish and chips during a discussion

on seven-year-old M, presenting with
pain down there (by his cousin),

taken into care after being removed
for witnessing Mum's self-immolation.

After, I wiped
the mushy peas from my mouth.

I donned mask, visor, and apron,
washed my hands the right way,

vaccinated death in a red dressing gown,
touched its eggshell, auscultated its yolk.

I have heard ghosts blooming like spring mist
through my stethoscope.

Dissection Room: Reproductive Anatomy

The demonstrator is
using a kebab skewer
to scrape past strings
of yellowed muscle,
tissue-paper intestines
and shredded labia.

He's hovering above
ovaries made raisins
by formaldehyde.
I am trying to focus
on fibrous ligaments
and their attachments,

but those wiry hairs
are really disconcerting,
and imaginary names
for her haunted eggs
jingle in my brain
like tiny bells. Poor thing,

I wish she had been
gifted to the maggots.
They know how to butcher
a body with reverence.

Aunty

He is bleeding out on the table.
She raises her scalpel, conducts
a fermata. The tent falls silent.
She sutures Death's open mouth,
her hand a flute for the wounded
charming Hope from its basket—

She convulses awake like a fish out its bowl, puts on slippers and
heads downstairs to prepare egg and soldiers while the kids change
into uniforms. He enters the kitchen, stamps her forehead with a kiss
before leaving for work. How easy it is to seal a mind shut and call
it love. She cannot count the years since he put her degrees in the
garage. *Better for now to keep them somewhere safe.* She waves him out
the driveway, garage keys in her dressing gown sleeve. Once he pulls
away, she's inside rummaging, frenzied as an archaeologist excavating
the fragments of her own life. She pauses. There it is, behind the paint
cans and bike pump, the cardboard box on a corner shelf. Delicately,
she prises it open. She lifts the unframed parchment to her lips as
if it were Scripture, dust brushing her mouth like powdered sugar.
She takes care to place her life back in the box, exactly as it was left.
Later, he dissects his day over the dinner she's made. He discusses his
difficult colleagues, gently scolds the kids for leaving their vegetables.
He reaches across the table, squeezes the hand that once amputated
all four limbs of a man in one night. *We can be a real family here, can't
we dear?*

Uncle

"O women! I have seen that the majority of the dwellers of Hellfire were you."
– Weak hadith

Uncle sits on the mosque committee
A position of great importance in our community
He was elected on a mandate of change
Though probably recognises the danger
Of being perceived as any kind of radical
When the mosque is still monitored by the council
Must be why they spent the money on air conditioning
Instead of the library we asked for

He is respectful
The type to place one hand on his heart and bow his head
When he sees you in the car park after taraweeh
So respectful he won't even look at his wife
Just the secretary he works with
Even after the brief fling in Madagascar
The mosque embraced him with an open-armed salaam
Who am I to judge the sins of man?

taraweeh – night-time congregational prayers in Ramadan
Weak hadith – hadith deemed unauthenticated by scholars, sometimes used to justify
personal or cultural positions in the name of religion

Religious Education

I

My feet do not reach the floor on a stranger's sofa. After-school light
paints squares on the walls. I read Qaida for the first time. My finger
swirls round the letter shapes like milk in a teacup.

II

I adjust my pull-over hijab in a car park the masjid shares with the
church. Inside, Ayesha warns me the devil lives under my fingernails.
Big Appa hits my sister with a plastic ruler. We giggle in straightened
rows when the Imam draws a blank during Sura Baqarah.

III

Ayesha's mum lets us read in her living room (nobody will tell us what
the Imam did wrong). We recite Quran in birdsong unison. There
is great outrage after Little Appa announces her cousin's gymnastic
routine as the winner of Mosque's Got Talent.

IV

Qari Saab perfects our tajweed. His fingers trace each line, leave
contrails across the sky of the page. For each mistake I stand up and
face the wall, shrink to a sukun.

V

Our replacement teaches Arabic from a pink cassette player. She
directs me to find ع at the base of my throat (as if I am coughing up
phlegm). She shows me a selfie of her cousin, he is queuing to confirm

Gaddafi's corpse is really dead. She bakes orange blossom cake when I complete the thirtieth chapter.

Appa – Urdu term for older sister
Qaida – a book used to teach children Quranic Arabic
Qari Saab – Arabic teacher
tajweed – set of rules for correct pronunciation of Quranic recitation
sukun – a diacritic used in Arabic to mark the absence of a vowel

Birthday Party

It was simpler to declare birthdays haram
than explain we cannot afford them,
so she took matters into her own hands.

That afternoon, a ribbon of plaited girls
gathered at the door holding gift-bags.
The party erupted like a piñata.

An older sister cursed, raiding the cupboards
for bread and jam, cut sandwiches
into finger-sized squares.

The younger sister wrapped a matchbox
in layers of yesterday's newspaper,
an impromptu pass-the-parcel.

Nobody could deny a party
when the guests were already knocking,
presents and cards in hand.

They bobbed in the hallway like waves,
a sea of whispers and awe,
as the birthday girl made her way downstairs

with self-braided hair
and a sequined kameez,
cheeks sparkling with smeared eyeshadow.

The children danced around cushions,
played musical chairs with the curtains drawn.
When they brought out the cake,

a Battenburg from the Irish neighbours,
her brother lit the candles with his pocket light.
The little girl twinkled in the dark,

as she whispered *bismillah*
before making a wish,
serenaded by a chorus of *hip hip hooray*!

Painting Faces

Mum takes the afternoon off work
to paint our faces for the school play.
She sweeps pink blush across my cheeks,
strokes tiny lines of white into feathers
on the delicate skin around my eyes.

She lifts up the mirror and I fizz like sherbet,
until I see Katie (my enemy) behind me
in the queue. I gesture in secret,
ask Mum to paint a spider on her face.
Only because Katie is a mean girl.

She only plays with other girls called Katie,
even if I ask nicely. So I call her *fish food*,
because of the flakes in her hair.
She never picks me for her team in PE,
says I am too fat to run, even though *she*
is the one who wants seconds at lunch!

Sitting on a stool, Mum gently presses
powdery glitter onto her eyelids.
Inside, I whistle furious as a kettle,
watch my mum tuck Katie's hair
behind her ears. She is making Katie laugh,

and Katie is behaving as if she's never heard
a joke before. Mum isn't even that funny.
My ears prickle like nettles as her long fingers
trace a line of sparkle above Katie's brow.
Katie, you look beautiful.

In the car on the way home,
Mum lauds my faultless range as Seagull
(in chorus) and Beachball Number Two.
I cross my arms, do not say a word.
Like a meteorologist, she detects
the storm cloud passing over my face.

You shouldn't have been so nice to her,
she is a nasty horrible girl, she never
remembers her lines her hair is always
greasy she – Mum pulls over, wipes the tears
off my face, fingers soothing as aloe.

I don't know if you noticed, but
nobody came to hear Katie's solo.
She doesn't have a mum
to care for her like you do.
The next day at lunch, Katie
is behind me in the queue.

Your mum is very pretty, she whispers.
I barely turn to face her.
I've seen her picking you up after school.
She said I can come to yours for dinner.
I roll a marble eye in her direction.
Can I still come? Please?

River

After Selima Hill

Other people's mothers
don't shout at them in public,
I cry in the car on the way
back from dinner.
Other people's mothers
don't cremate their
daughters with a look.
My mother opens
like the seed of a tree.

I am sorry, she says.
You are right. But
other people's mothers
had the chance
to be daughters.
Other people's mothers
were softened by rivers.
I had to be bedrock
all my life.

I am sorry
you can feel silt
in my love,
but know you are
water to me.
Wherever you run
I'll run under you,
holding the current
like no one else can.

Umma's Kitchen

I watch you through a fog
of onion tears, our noses fizz with mirch
and garam masala. I suggest paprika.

You wipe away my tears, hands soft as kajoor,
the trace of chilli on your fingertips
sears my eye. I see you in red,

but you are, and will always be, lilac
like the chaadar you wear over your silver hair,
the lavender you plant between weeds.

Once the hissing oil begins to whisper,
you slice garlic (with care) into the haandi,
then lift the wooden spoon to my mouth.

My eyes give me away – too much mirch.
You laugh. Your silly English granddaughter
can't handle the Pakistani heat.

Umma – paternal grandmother
mirch – chilli
kajoor – dates
chaadar – shawl or large scarf
haandi – metal pot used for cooking

Nanny's Tupperware

I peer at you through a lid
that doesn't fit the box
you handed me. I cannot
see the shape of you, the lid
is clouded from years of filling,
emptying, washing, reusing.
This box has lived many lives.
Now it holds the wooden beads
of a broken tasbeeh, each a prayer
waiting to be restrung.

They sleep next to the soil
of Karbala, which you press
against your forehead because
Imam Ali's warmth means
you don't need to turn
the heating on. Still, it's cold
inside this kitchen where you
thread your beads. I pick one,
stare at you through the hole.
Hard, round, empty without string.

tasbeeh – prayer beads

For Poppo

January 1970–March 1970

You were a sigh of relief,
    soft hands with tiny nails

my grandmother could paint,
    petal breath, cheeks in violet bloom.

I wonder if they saw you
    when they first saw me, held me

like a light bulb unscrewed
    from the sky, hot hands holding hot glass.

You went undocumented,
    a thumbprint in a photo album,

blank pages in a passport,
    sent across etch-a-sketch borders.

I think about the atta
    your hands never had to knead,

words you couldn't yell in fights
    with brothers you never knew,

lipstick you never got to smudge,
    love you never grieved in secret.

You, a song,
    on the tip of a tongue.

Poppo – paternal aunt

Asr Prayer

You arrive at the airport
with a suitcase full of American goods:
M&Ms, watches, hairdryers.

Your cousins pull you into a playful chokehold,
rub their knuckles against your scalp like flint.
Young girls glance at you a moment longer

than they should, wilt into women
as you move through the street, your green eyes
lighting the way like fireflies.

Your aunties have made fresh roti
and are milling you as you enter the house,
our Amreekan boy has come home.

Your cousins do not take you for a drive.
Instead, you go for a swim in the Swat River,
your skin like olive oil in the water.

Your cousins look upon your beauty and say *mashallah.*
They give you a towel, dry clothes, walk you home safely.
They do not take you for a drive.

They do not crash the car and carry your body
back through the village, shrouded in a leather jacket.
Your cousins do not take you for a drive.

They drop you at the airport, where you give them
your salaam. You land safely. Your mother holds
her precious boy and you hold her back.

You finish school, attend college.
Your brother learns to cook, not cage-fight,
because your brother isn't angry.

You marry and we steal your shoes at the wedding.
On Eid, you walk into the garden with a wife
and a baby. Your grandmother

kisses you on the forehead.
You are
her loveliest one.

Asr – one of the five daily prayers and the title of Surah 103 in the Quran (translates as The
Declining Day)

Fresh Off the Boat

Not enough life jackets,
he gives the last one to his sister
who clutches his leg, his body a raft.
By the time he makes it to shore,
her lungs are full of salt and ice.
He holds her limp body all night
as they sway in the van like cattle.

At night he stands frying chicken
in the back of a shop for rowdy teens,
who spit out his country on a list
of places the UK should invade,
to the soundtrack of golden oil
splashing. He smirks, they're so drunk
they don't realise they already have.
His boss flashes a traffic light eye,
reminds him of his pending status.

When I teach the proper vocab
for clothing, his eyes are nets,
catching what swims at them,
his hands driftwood when he
holds out a phone, asks please
if I call him sometime. I can't,
I'm only his teacher. He nods.
It's just I have same name as his sister,
and this country is cold, and my voice
is like, and he points to the board,
blanket.

Timeline

regional accent is crying in the beach hut
she has just been properly mugged off

influencer is offering you laxative
branded as flat tummy tea for the summer
#sponsored #ad

Breaking News: Foreign Body Drowned
Crossing the Mediterranean

influencer is offering you gummy bear vitamins
for hair as soft as her extensions
#sponsored #ad

Union Jack is rejoicing
illegals cannot claim benefits
when they are dead

blonde highlights is elbowing the air
in a car park to film a dance for TikTok

[uncredited photograph]
child with seaweed in hair and blue skin
is lying on sand next to litter

blonde highlights is live-streaming herself
crying on the living room floor,
she is so sorry she was just miming the lyrics

regional accent is posting a no-makeup selfie
to #raiseawareness for the ongoing crisis

Google is showing results for the movie Titanic
based on your most recent search:
boat, tragedy

The last man on Earth

begins solitude by relishing his freedoms.
New-found proprietor of every landfill,
he gloats, proud as the one chosen first
from the queue of lambs lining up for the abattoir,
crowns himself king for an empire of one.
When the ocean coughs up a new shoal of oil-slick fish,
he feels justified in naming their corpses after himself.
Has he not earned the right to inherit the Earth?
Has he not hustled, in spite of warnings
from the papers and protestors, his way
to accumulating all that the world has to offer?
If it takes setting the planet on fire to up his stock price,
he knows that in business, it's every man for himself.
When retirement comes sooner than planned,
he treks the whole Trans-Siberian railway
just to spot trains that lay crashed off the tracks.
He collects bricks from the collapsed Great Wall,
plays a jumbo-sized game of solo Jenga.
With a Swiss army knife, he carves out the face
of Mona Lisa, turns her into a photo stand-in.
He wanders round derelict shopping malls,
tries on wigs and prom dresses to re-enact
makeover montage scenes from the movies.
Though he never tires of graffitiing statements
about the size of his manhood on every billboard,
it isn't long before the piles of dead bodies
rotting on each street corner start to creep him out.
He was never the spiritual type, but he swears
sometimes, he can hear them groaning his name.
One morning, a corpse strewn in parts

across the pavement points its flesh-eaten finger
towards him. He tells himself it's a trick of the light.
More and more he keeps to his library, sleeps
behind a makeshift trench of stacked thesauruses.
Since the supply to demand ratio of buttons
has never been better, he crafts sock puppets,
and recreates his favourite childhood stories.
Eventually, he'll retreat to a church in the woods,
drop to his knees in the confessional booth.
But there'll come no pardon from the father,
palms pressed stone in rigor mortis prayer.

Taxi Driver

I am relieved to see a tasbeeh
hanging behind the air freshener.
After exchanging niceties and village names,
he tells me the story he cannot forget

> At school there was a girl who dated a gora,
> and, of course, we knew
> but nobody said anything,
> in case the girl's brothers found out,
> because in those days, they'd kill him on sight.
> Anyway, she was his girlfriend
> and one day I heard him in the playground,
> talking to his mates about her,
> you know, how boys do, and he says to his mates
> that he's seeing a paki. Later that day
> he went to kiss her behind the bins,
> and after, winked at his mates.

He glances at me through the rear-view mirror

> Do you understand, puttar?
> It doesn't matter whether you
> drive their cabs, or cure their cancer.
> There is no we. Only us. And them.

gora – Urdu for white person
puttar – Punjabi for son/daughter

Breakfast with Nanny

The clock spasms all day
around half past three

Toast glints with melted ghee
next to tablets on a porcelain plate

The cereal bowls are still in wudhu
radio fragments stud the silence

Asians ought to

Back in my day

You can't say anything these days

without being labelled a

I lean against the sink and twist
the dial until static crackles

You ask why I turn it off
I ask why you listen

Sunlight runs through
the troubled threads of your eyes

It helps me improve my English

wudhu – ritual washing before prayer

But where are you really from?

Clay. A shapeshifting clot of blood. A kernel inside the first shell-breath of God. Primordial soup, reduced to its atoms after being brought to boil. The same place as the stars and birds, where everything that ever existed was wrapped in tin foil and microwaved into being. An iron ballerina, pirouetting round the Sun and sweating out the Oceans. Mountains formed in an ice tray mould. A patch of grass that drifted from elsewhere. A patch of grass still drifting. Like a refugee with amnesia, I cannot recall home, though once in a while, I catch its fragrance on the wind.

Ghazal

After Mona Arshi

If what we share turns water to ink,
Even the oceans would disappear.

At night, we dissolve cartographers' maps,
Let the borders between us disappear.

Gift me your rib, and I'll play Eve,
Until the colours of Paradise disappear.

My name is like sherbet on your lips,
One drop of rain and I disappear.

I've become a lighthouse, beaming you back,
In dark, you always disappear.

For you, I'd halve my heart in brine,
Is it better to pickle or disappear?

I'll perfume my wrists for the funeral pyre,
Unmoth your eye and disappear!

While I reincarnate as smoke, be breeze,
Dance with me, before I disappear.

Third Date

I made the day a snow globe.

There we are,
tiny figurines at the top of Carlton Hill
dancing hands frozen mid-air
your head tilted back, forever
suspended in slow glitter.

If I tried,
I could hold the whole sky
between my thumb and index finger,
shake us upside down until
snow falls
        from our feet.

Honeymoon for One

I nearly drowned treading water   in the ocean you promised me
A wave offered me up to the shore   like a prayer trapped in plastic
I made a roof from the veil   a dreamcatcher from my bangled wrists

Castaways are   by nature   resourceful

I make fires with flint fingers   write poems in the sand
Hold myself   the way milk is held by coconut husk
After dreams of you I lift a conch shell to my ear   *this will pass*

Last night I saw   tourists with binoculars on a catamaran
This morning an ogling fisherman   I imagine him carving me
Into wood as myth   the jilted bride whose eyes turned to sea urchins

Consider this   my message in a bottle:

I am alone and alive
My soul does not need saving

Acknowledgements

This small collection would not have been possible without the huge support of an incredible group of people.

I owe everything I have and am to my parents. Mum, thank you for loving me enough to show me my soul; Abu, thank you for being my example of compassion. Bijan, thank you for being my creative mentor – I owe all my ideas to you. Alina, thank you for being my unofficial editor and official ride-or-die. To my grandparents, thank you for teaching me the soul of poetry before I learned its body.

All credit is due to the amazing team at The Poetry Business, especially Suzannah, for your kindness, sensitivity, and expert skill in editing these poems. Extra shout out to Katie for bearing with my neurotic adjustments to the cover design (only to have me return to the original). Thank you to Kim Moore for judging my pamphlet worthy of publication, and also to the Arvon Foundation and Green Templeton College, whose generosity allowed me to put it together.

I wrote my first 'proper' poem in an Arvon workshop with Peter Sansom. If it wasn't for your continued support and interest in my work, it would have been my last. Thank you to Ann and Peter Sansom for your constant wisdom and encouragement. Warda Yassin, my poetry sister, you are truly that girl and have set *thee* standard for Muslim women creatives. Andy Wildin, my sixth-form English teacher, thank you for introducing me to Grace Nichols and for teaching me the word 'post-colonial' – everything here started in those lessons. I began creative writing with Doncaster Young Writers and Hive South Yorkshire, led by Vicky Morris. Like countless other young people whose lives you have touched with your tireless enthusiasm and care, Vicky, I write because of you.

Thank you to my beautiful friends, who have held me while I ugly cried and laughed with me until I almost peed in the street. Special thanks to Sara Yassi, whose 3am notes are the reason this collection exists today.

Ultimately, all praise is due to Allah – any beauty within these pages belongs to Him and every mistake is my own.